Introduction

Recently I overheard the following conversation between a man and a woman in a local café. I assumed they were long-time partners (I could have been wrong, but I don't think so)...

Her: Will you stop going on about it? I didn't even mark the bumper.

Him: That's not the point. Either you didn't look or you're useless at judging distances.

Her: I can judge distances as well as you can –

Him: (*interrupting*) Then you didn't look. You never look! For goodness' sake there was plenty of room to back into that parking space.

Her: You can talk – you nearly got yourself run over on Saturday crossing the road!

Him: (*irritated*) There was nothing coming.

Her: Obviously there was because it nearly hit you.

Him: What's that got to do with your useless parking? That's typical; instead of admitting fault, you either change the subject or try to pick at somebody else!

Her: I'm not picking on you. I'm saying that nobody's perfect, OK.

Him: (*with some heat*) Yeah, well you know what makes perfect – practice!

Her: Yeah, well you should practise being a bit more tolerant.

Him: (*intolerantly*) Oh that's rich coming from you. What about last week when...

But then their meals arrived and I didn't manage to catch any more. However, even that short segment was interesting. What struck me was how quickly the argument developed and the way it fed off itself. The only direction the conversation was moving in was towards more argument. It also seemed very well rehearsed, in that it followed a familiar course. It came out of nowhere and neither person seemed to notice that; nor did either of them seem at any point to stand back from the argument and ask 'What's happening? Why am I letting myself be like this?'

This type of quarrel is like a pinball game, where the topic of conversation is bounced around in a bad-tempered point-scoring contest, until it drops at last and inevitably into the black hole of bad feeling. I can remember many times when I've had similar exchanges with my wife or other family members or friends. And, I can see now how negative and unnecessary those quarrels had been. But as we all know, it's easy to have 20/20 vision in hindsight. The trick is to have that clear perception and clear thinking in the *present moment*, so that you can change the course of events. That is emotional intelligence, and that is what this book is about.

Howard Gardner, an important figure in developing some of the insights of emotional intelligence (see for example *Multiple Intelligences: the Theory in Practice*), highlights the notion that 'intelligence' is our innate capability to handle information – to manipulate it and exploit it beneficially: we are all equipped with the potential to handle information in many ways.

Emotional intelligence encompasses 'intrapersonal intelligence' – our ability to handle information about our own thoughts, feelings and physical behaviours; and 'interpersonal intelligence' (people skills) – our ability to handle situations involving others more artfully and positively, turning lose-lose pinball games into win-win scenarios.

Implicit in this book is the idea that the students themselves are the resource for developing their own emotional intelligence: the qualities are latent in us all. As teachers, we can only draw these out in our students; we cannot force them in. As the wise saying goes,

> 'My teacher showed me the gateway, but I entered by myself.'

Being emotionally intelligent

Concept

Intelligence, resourcefulness and literacy

Emotional intelligence (EI) is also called emotional resourcefulness. We are, or can become, resourceful in the sense that we use certain resources to achieve our aims. But what are these things that we 're-source', that we go back to again and again as the source of our ability to handle feelings in ourselves and in others? I believe they stem from four main areas:

Developing sensory acuity
Using our senses with greater awareness and more acutely to become increasingly perceptive.

Developing the ability to change our mental-emotional state
Doing this means being able to 'catch ourselves' in the heat of the moment so that we can make decisions there and then about what we think and how we feel. An important part of this is knowledge of relaxation techniques.

Developing responsibility – the ability we have to respond
This involves the points above and the capacity to think clearly and flexibly. That in turn requires

Developing a creative attitude
Creativity can usefully be considered as a way of turning information into 'in-formation', into the active formation of greater understanding.

Another term for EI is 'emotional literacy'. If we define literacy as an ability to read and write, then emotional literacy amounts to the skill we can bring to bear in reading other people's emotions and writing our own emotional 'scripts' – creating new and more positive templates for the way we think, feel and behave.

> 'For the uncontrolled there is no wisdom,
> nor for the uncontrolled is there the power of
> concentration; and where there is no concentration
> there is no peace. And for the unpeaceful,
> how can there be happiness?'
> *Bhagavad Gita*

Application

These questions act as a gateway into the field of EI. Think about them for yourself and encourage your students to consider them. If you are working with younger children, you will need to rephrase the questions to some extent.

1. When was the last time you experienced an unpleasant emotion or feeling? What do you think caused it?
2. When was the last time you experienced a pleasant emotion? Again, what caused it?
3. How do you feel right now? Notice your body posture and any points of physical tension.
4. How do you feel generally? Are you happy and contented or worried and frustrated most of the time? Why do you think this is so?
5. When you are in a good mood, do you do anything to maintain it? If not, what could you do to sustain those good feelings?
6. Think back to the 'pinball argument' (see p3). When were you last in that kind of situation? What caused the quarrel? Using 20/20 hindsight, what could you have done to change the scenario?
7. Think about somebody you like and with whom you get on well. Notice the feelings that accompany the memories. What is it about this person that contributes to this positive relationship? What is it about you that contributes to this positive relationship?
8. Think about somebody you dislike. Notice the feelings that accompany the memories. What is it about this person, and what is it about you, that contributes to this negative relationship? Now, to clear away any unpleasant memories, think of someone you do like!
9. What do you do to relax and unwind?
10. On a scale of 1–5, how much do you think you are in control of your own thoughts and feelings?

Concept

The mind-body link

The mind and the body are fundamentally linked. What we think – and how we think – has a direct bearing on how we feel, which in turn influences our physical state. Catching our minds in action and noticing the flow of thoughts, creates the opportunity to change them. This gives us greater control over our emotional map. Training our thinking makes us better map makers!

This insight highlights the relationship between awareness, understanding and control. When we are more aware of our thoughts and feelings, we understand more deeply how they are connected to our whole emotional and physical being. Deeper understanding leads to greater control. Over time, this establishes a positive feedback loop within ourselves that makes us more emotionally resourceful.

Memory is an important tool in the mind-body link. 'To remember' literally means 'to bring back to the members' – to re-create in the body the feelings that were originally linked to the memory. To remember is to re-create very powerfully the original experience.

> **TIP:**
> Metaphors, such as 'landscape' and 'map', are useful to help visualize subtle and intangible notions such as concepts, thoughts and feelings. Other metaphors I've found helpful are 'orchestra', 'garden', and 'captain and crew' to help describe the conscious and subconscious parts of the mind. Make a note of other metaphors that resonate for you.

Application

- Ask your students to remember times that made them feel good. Do these memories now bring back those pleasant emotions?
- Now ask your students to imagine situations that haven't occurred – or maybe never will – which evoke those same feelings (a student in one workshop I ran imagined flying on the back of Pegasus the winged horse to re-create in herself a feeling of exhilaration).

Concept

Conscious and subconscious thinking

The idea of the subconscious (or unconscious) part of the mind is no longer new. Eminent thinkers such as Sigmund Freud and Carl Jung developed it as a key aspect of their theories of how the human mind works and it is now generally accepted that our minds are endlessly busy at a level beyond the realm of conscious awareness.

Any attempt to explore the concept briefly is bound to be simplistic. However, it is important to touch upon the notion as it has a practical value in developing EI. Conscious thinking occurs 'out in the open'. We are aware of our conscious thoughts as they happen, and we usually know why we are thinking them. We can also change those thoughts simply by deciding to do so.

Subconscious thinking happens 'behind the scenes'. Links, associations and meanings are being made largely without our knowing about it. What we consciously think and experience becomes woven into our map of memory and then influences our perception of the world. Very often, limiting behaviour, such as lack of confidence, has its roots in subconscious memories.

Exploring the subconscious origins of limiting behaviour requires specialized techniques. However, we can immediately apply the key principle that what we consciously attend to, we subconsciously react to.

Application

- Begin by becoming increasingly aware of your students' language. Notice any limiting language they use relating to their own capabilities. Words such as 'can't', 'won't', 'shouldn't', 'never' and other absolutes are often failures of imagination or nerve rather than a lack of ability. Notice also any metaphors that inhibit a student's development and then make the student aware of it. For example, if a student says 'Trying to understand this work is an uphill struggle', you can say 'Well, pretend you're riding a trail bike as you understand the work'; this broadens the metaphor of an 'uphill struggle' in a more positive and empowering way. Such rewording of language is not being frivolous or just playing with words. What we consciously imagine influences our subconscious perceptions of ourselves and the world: this engages with deep-rooted (often negative) subconscious perceptions that can limit our behaviour.

- This technique often works well in dealing with apprehension and worry. Ask your students to think about a past or anticipated experience that worries them. They imagine they are watching this as a video replay on a TV, for which they have the remote control. As the event appears in their minds' eye, the students play-and-fast-forward to the end of the event; then play-and-rewind to the beginning. They do this several times. Finally, the students 'step into' the scene as it plays-fast-forward-and-rewind. Repeat this several times until they feel that the imagined incident no longer troubles them so much, or at all. End by jumping out of the TV and pressing the remote's 'Off' button.

Controlling the speed at which the event is replayed modifies the memory and scrambles the way the brain has encoded the original experiences. The re-encoded information from this conscious observation and control re-sets our map of reality at a subconscious level.

Concept

Positive intentions

The principle of positive intentions is a powerful one in helping to develop greater emotional resourcefulness. Imagine inadvertently resting your hand on a very hot radiator. It burns – it hurts! And you snatch your hand away quickly. The pain was unpleasant, but the positive intention behind the pain was to minimize the damage to your hand. There is also the longer-term benefit of making you think before putting your hand on a radiator in future.

What we consciously think about, we subconsciously react to. If we deliberately think about the possible positive intentions behind perceived 'negative' emotions, we increase the likelihood that those emotions will moderate or fade, to be replaced by a more positive intention.

TIP:
You might choose to begin by exploring these emotions in a general way, rather than asking students to talk about specific personal experiences. For instance, how might we use the feeling of jealousy in a positive way? How can we use that seemingly negative emotion to drive us in a more constructive direction? Maybe jealousy focuses my mind on things I want but haven't got. Perhaps it would help to re-examine my values. If I still want those things I haven't got, can the feeling of jealousy motivate me to work out some practical and emotionally safe strategies for getting them?

Application

- Point out to students the etymological link between the words emotions, motives and movement (actions). Our feelings drive us to act. But we do not need to be the passive victims of the way we feel.
- Encourage students to develop an awareness of the positive intentions that can be realized from what are usually thought of as negative or unpleasant emotions.

Concept

Mapping emotions

Human beings are capable of experiencing a vast range of emotions. Becoming more aware of our amazing potential to have these feelings brings them more under our conscious scrutiny and control.

Our feelings are generated by how each of us *perceives* what happens. We make ourselves angry, happy or envious, and so on. These feelings exist in us, not in the things that happen.

ANGER

jealousy

HAPPINESS

JOY

sadness

anxiety

fear

Application

- Make a checklist of all the emotions you can think of. Use a thesaurus to help you.
- Pick an emotion to explore – for example 'annoyance'. Ask students to describe briefly on scraps of paper something that annoys them. Pass the scraps around and ask each student to give the experience a rating on a 1–5 scale – 1 is mildly annoying and 5 is intensely annoying. If appropriate, ask students to talk about why they gave the rating for that experience. Students will learn that what greatly annoys one person hardly bothers someone else.
- Talk about the differences between similar emotions. How is envy different from jealousy, for instance? Is irritation the same as annoyance? How does happiness feel – and how does joy feel?
- Make an Emotions Matrix (see below). The lower half of the vertical axis is for negative emotions and the upper half is for positive ones. The horizontal axis plots the increasing rarity with which emotions are experienced. Groups of students decide together where to plot chosen emotions on the matrix – this can lead to interesting discussions.

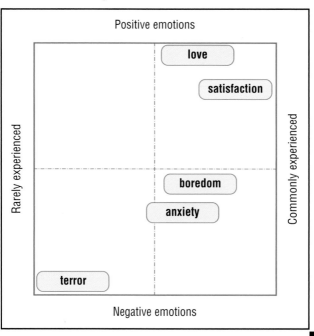

Concept

Self-sabotage

It's easy to allow negative patterns of thinking to develop. If these patterns go unrecognized they allow unhelpful negative feelings to become our automatic response to life's experiences. Such patterns are called *cognitive distortions*. Some of the more common ones are...

All-or-nothing thinking

Things are seen in black and white. If something isn't perfect then it's a total disaster.

Over-generalization

Amplifying a single negative event into a general principle or into an ongoing escalating crisis.

What-if worrying

Worrying about events that haven't happened and may never happen.

Labelling

Putting a mental label on yourself or someone else. These are usually negative labels such as 'I'm just a loser' or 'He's a complete idiot'.

Negative filtering

Picking out the negative aspects of an experience and failing (or refusing) to see the positive aspects.

Personalization

Taking the blame for things, whether or not that blame exists or is justified.

See my book *Self-Intelligence* for more about cognitive distortions and ways of developing EI.

Application

- Explain one or more cognitive distortions to your students and ask them to recall any occasions when they've fallen into that pattern of thinking. If appropriate, invite them to talk about these experiences.
- Find proverbs that reflect cognitive distortions. Encourage students to make up new proverbs focusing on the positive. So, for example…
  - 'It never rains but it pours' – an all-or-nothing/over generalization
    New proverb – 'The sun never comes out but it shines all day.'
  - 'The fool and his money are soon parted' – labelling/what-if worrying
    New proverb – 'The wise person saves and spends carefully.'
  - 'A hungry man is an angry man' – negative filtering
    New proverb – 'A hungry man searches more cleverly for food.'
- Students create posters, badges and stickers that help to break negative patterns of thinking. For example…
  - What-if may never happen!
  - Worrying is like riding a rocking horse. You work hard at it but get nowhere.
  - Blame is the weapon of the weak.
  - Whatever's happened, you've survived.

TIP:
There are plenty of useful sayings in reference books and on internet sites of quotes…
- 'The only high road to success is failure.' *R.L. Stevenson*
- 'The person who can't make a mistake can't make anything.' *Abraham Lincoln*
- 'Someone who carries his own lantern has no need to fear the dark.' *Chinese proverb*

How to chill out

Concept

2

Relaxation is…

Because the mind and the body are linked, true relaxation involves both. Sitting quietly, feeling physically rested while your mind is whirling trying to solve a number of problems is not relaxation!

We all have the potential to relax, but learning to do so is a skill. Perhaps especially in our busy, competitive, achievement-oriented culture, the notion of simply doing nothing might be frowned upon. However, if we think of relaxation time as 'recharging the batteries' ready for further action, perhaps the idea is not so contentious.

The realization that has evolved in recent decades that every aspect of our psychobiology is periodic is of great significance (Rossi, 1993). Throughout the day we experience spans of high alertness and concentration followed by lulls or troughs where we naturally tune out; attention tends to defocus and turn inward; we detach more from the activity of the outside world and let our thoughts drift. This is the so-called ultradian rhythm, a cycle that averages around 90 minutes. It is a rhythm that may also affect the brain's hemispheric dominance (research shows that different brain hemispheres have different qualities – right is predominantly intuitive, left is predominantly logical), and the functioning of the body's autonomic systems.

The implications for education are immense and, to date, relatively unexplored. However, encouraging and teaching students to relax – and if possible building relaxation time into the school day – may go some way towards exploiting what we need to do naturally to be at our best.

Application

■ Discuss the notion of relaxation with your students. Point out that true relaxation involves both the physical and mental aspects of a person. Encourage students to investigate relaxation techniques (some of which are outlined in Section 2). Raise the issue of relaxation time with colleagues. Could the learning of relaxation techniques become incorporated into the curriculum?

■ Ask students to collect examples of visuals they find relaxing, such as countryside scenes, quiet shorelines, woodland – and build a resource bank of soothing music. Relaxing sound effects, such as water lapping on the shore and birdsong are readily available on CDs.

■ Collect phrases and sayings that highlight the idea and encourage the ethos of relaxation, such as:
  – 'Sitting quietly doing nothing,
    Spring comes and the grass grows by itself'
    a well-known Zen adage.
  – 'Sometimes I sits and thinks. And sometimes I just sits...'.
    seen on a poster depicting the musings of a character propped comfortably against a tree.

■ As far as possible, begin each lesson with a short period of relaxation. Couple this with the techniques we are about to explore...

Concept

Self-noticing

Relaxation is, for most people, not something that happens by default. Very often even when we're sitting quietly supposedly relaxing, shoulders can be hunched, fingers might be clenched, breathing could be relatively shallow and rapid. And it's so easy for our thoughts to drift idly towards worry – which of course increases physical tension immediately.

Many people are habitually tense and never realize it. Self-noticing – catching ourselves in this state which is not relaxation – is the first step towards doing something about it.

TIP:
Remember to practise what you preach. Notice any points of tension in yourself. Model as many of the relaxation and EI techniques in this book as possible.

Application

Point out to students that negative thoughts create physical tension and kick-start the 'worry reaction', a repeating pattern of negative thoughts, physical tension and accompanying unpleasant emotions. With the students sitting quietly, ask them to notice…

- if they are frowning – 'Smooth out those frown lines.'
- if their teeth are clenched – ' Relax the jaw.'
- if shoulders are hunched – 'Shrug your shoulders and then let them drop.'
- if the posture is hunched or slumped – 'Sit up (not with military straightness) but with the head balanced easily and naturally above the spine.'
- if fists are clenched – 'Open out the fingers. Let the hands rest, palms up, in the lap.'
- if breathing is shallow and rapid – 'Slow and deepen the breathing cycle.'
- if stomach muscles are tight – 'Let the stomach drop.'
- if feet are twitching or tapping – 'Conserve your energy and let yourself become still.'
- if thoughts wander towards worrying – 'Gently but firmly bring the thoughts back to body-awareness.'

I'm not doing anything.
I must be relaxed!

Concept

Relaxation and breathing

Breathing is one of the bodily functions that occurs automatically and unconsciously (largely without our being aware of it), but which we can bring under conscious control at any time. Blinking is another such process. We can go through the entire day and fail to notice that we have been blinking every few moments. However, we can choose to take over our blinking at will (not that we'd particularly want to).

Because breathing is deeply linked to the rest of our physiology, it forms an effective way of relaxing ourselves. When we choose to control our breathing and use it to settle and quieten, the rest of the body follows and our thoughts will become calmer too.

During any breathing exercise, remind students to stop if they feel light-headed or dizzy, and to breathe normally. If you think that a student is starting to hyperventilate, get them to breathe into a paper bag held gently over the nose and mouth.

TIP:
Some students might feel self-conscious or silly doing these breathing techniques. Discourage teasing and where possible encourage students to practise with their eyes gently closed or to face away from each other. Model the techniques yourself (having tried them out beforehand so that you know how they work).

Application

1. Deepening the breath

Students sit upright but 'loose' on their chairs, with their hands resting palms up in their laps, as they would after the 'self-noticing' activity (see p19). Ask them to slow their breathing, making sure they don't hunch or raise their shoulders during the in-breath. Now ask the students to breathe deliberately from the stomach, rather than from the chest – the stomach bulges out on the inhale and it draws in on the exhale. Do this slowly, repeating the cycle about six times.

These breathing and relaxation techniques work best if students breathe through the nose; however, if this is not possible, the exercises will still be effective.

2. Rhythmic breathing

Having practised exercise 1, go through the breathing cycle in this way:
- inhale to a slow count of four (you can count aloud while the students pace their breathing)
- hold the breath for six
- exhale to a slow count of four.

Repeat the cycle three or four times. Remind students to breathe normally if they feel uncomfortable.

3. White light – blue light breathing

Once students have mastered slower, deeper, more controlled breathing, ask them to imagine a white light full of energy streaming into their bodies as they inhale, and a blue light, full of the stresses and cares of the day, flowing outwards as they exhale. Repeat the cycle up to six times. Even if the students are not predominantly visual thinkers, ask them to imagine the white and blue light in whatever way is most effective for them.

Concept

Cat waking up

Legend has it that the basic postures of physical yoga (Hatha) evolved out of people watching a cat as it woke, stretched, arched its back and preened itself, then curled up to go back to sleep. Incidentally, Hatha yoga and its associated practice of meditation remains one of the most effective and beneficial ways known of improving mental, emotional and physical health and well-being (see *Helping Children with Yoga* by Sarah Woodhouse and Michelle Cheesbrough for further information).

Consider trying to establish a yoga class in school taught by a qualified yoga teacher. Contact the British Wheel of Yoga for information on teachers in your area.

While even a basic outline of yoga techniques are beyond the scope of this book, we can use some of its simpler insights to improve our students' ability to relax.

Application

- Ask students to mime or role-play a cat waking up and stretching itself, arching its back, then curling up again to sleep.
- Combine a visualization of clouds with suitable music and the breathing techniques discussed on p21.
- Develop the role-play idea by asking students to imagine and mime, for instance, clouds drifting by or ripe wheat waving gently in the breeze.
- Play some relaxing instrumental music to which students improvise movements – perhaps there is a dance and drama specialist in the school who could support you in this.
- If students have been sitting and concentrating for a long time, encourage them to yawn and stretch. Many schools teach students methods such as Brain Gym® (Dennison, 1987) and accelerated learning (Smith, 2002) and create opportunities for students to refresh themselves prior to further learning.

Concept

Visualization

Thoughts, feelings and physical states and reactions are all connected. When we deliberately alter the way we breathe or change our bodily posture and movement, we influence the flow of ideas through the mind. Similarly, knowingly shaping and directing our thoughts can have a profound and immediate impact on the way we feel and the degree of physical relaxation we can achieve.

Visualization techniques are safe, simple and versatile. They can be used across the age and ability range and are effective whatever a student's learning style and preferences. We can all visualize; we can all picture things in the mind's eye.

Application

1. Controlling visualization

Show students a simple object such as a plain white cup and saucer. Keep it in sight for half a minute or so and then put it away. Now ask the students to close their eyes or, if they prefer, gaze at a blank area of the wall (some students might want to look down at the table top or floor – that's fine). Ask them to visualize the cup and saucer and hold it in their mind's eye unwaveringly for 30 seconds – increase this concentration time progressively if you practise the technique regularly. Now ask the students to visualize changes to the cup and saucer – such as changing its size, shape, colour and pattern. Visualize it floating up in the air (a flying saucer!) and settling somewhere else. Fill it with different liquids. Imagine it made of different substances and materials. Play with the visualization for around five minutes.

2. Gathering helpful resources

Discuss with students personal qualities and feelings that count as positive helpful resources – such as a sense of humour, tolerance, higher self-esteem, increased self-confidence and determination. Pick one of these and ask students to imagine it as, for instance, a piece of fruit that they can now eat, or a badge that they can wear, or an ointment that they can absorb through the skin. Encourage students to experience the feelings those resources evoke as the visualization progresses.

3. Reframing negative experiences

It isn't necessary for students to remember negative experiences to do this visualization. Ask them to pretend that the experience they want to work with is recorded on a video tape. Imagine playing the tape on fast-forward so that images flicker meaninglessly on the screen. Now play and rewind at super speed. Go through this whole cycle many times for one minute. End with a calming breathing exercise. The fast forward-fast-rewind technique scrambles the way information has been previously encoded (remembered) and acts as an instruction for subconscious change.

Concept

A special place

Visualizing is a skill that can be developed to a high degree of sophistication. With some practise most students should be able to concentrate inwardly and in great detail for sustained periods of time. It also becomes possible then to build complex and powerful visualizations that have an immensely calming and empowering effect on the individual.

A particularly beneficial visualization is that of the 'special place' or 'safe haven'. This is how it works...

TIP:
If a student says 'I can't do that', reply by saying 'Well, just pretend you can and tell me when you've done it'. That usually gets the desired result.

Application

- Having previously practised relaxation and visualization techniques with your students, ask them now to imagine a place that's pleasant and comfortable; somewhere they can enjoy and where they feel safe.
- Encourage students to imagine this place in a multisensory way: imagine colours, sounds, smells and textures.
- As students imagine the safe, pleasant place, guide them through the Gathering helpful resources activity (see p25); thus they come to associate good and empowering feelings with their special place.
- The beneficial effects of the visualization are cumulative, so either revisit the activity regularly in class, or encourage students to do it for themselves in their own time.

I suggest combining the 'special place' visualization with anchoring techniques, about which you can learn more on p52.

3

Developing the senses

Concept

Active noticing

Dale Carnegie, in his excellent book *How to Win Friends and Influence People*, recounts the tale of a successful and popular businessman who was once asked if he was so well liked because he knew the first names of ten thousand employees, friends and acquaintances. 'No,' the man replied, 'I put my success down to the fact that I know the first names of **thirty** thousand employees, friends and acquaintances…'

This is an exceptional feat indeed: we can start more modestly. My wife always impresses me when, as we're passing through a supermarket checkout, she'll say to the checkout girl 'Oh, I like your earrings. Where did you get them?'. (She tends not to say it quite so often to the checkout boys!) Or, if the person looks tired, she'll notice that and say 'Long day?'. Or if she meets a friend she hasn't seen for a long time, she'll ask about the children or the pet cat, or say 'And did you manage to go on that holiday abroad you were so looking forward to?'.

This is, you'll appreciate, not about false flattery or small talk. And it's more than just being nosy. The fact is that people appreciate the attention. To truly attend to someone or something is a skill, a very valuable social skill, and one that needs to be practised and cultivated.

Application

- Change something about your classroom each day, such as a poster or an ornament. You don't have to tell the students – it's more enjoyable for them when they notice for themselves.

- Model active noticing yourself. Observing the changed position of the bookmark in a novel that a student is reading creates the opportunity for a teacher to say, 'You've certainly done plenty of reading this week. Is it a good book? Would you recommend it to me?'. Being aware of the tired and dispirited look in a student's eyes, even if you say nothing, allows you to interact with that student more beneficially.

- Teach your students some strategies for developing memory. There are many books on this subject: Tony Buzan (see References, p96) has written several excellent ones.

- Prepare – or ask the students to prepare – short video clips with some subsequent questions that test the class's observational skills.

- Apply active noticing to the material of your subject area. Link exploration of text, for instance, to thinking skills such as analysing for bias and assumption, speculation, interpretation and the use of metaphor and emotive language (see for instance *Teach Them Thinking* by Bellanca and Fogarty or my own book, *100 Ideas For Teaching Thinking Skills*).

Concept

Book and cover

'Never judge a book by its cover' is a saying that's hackneyed but nonetheless wise. Many years ago when I was shopping in town, a great booming voice from across the street called out my name. I (and several hundred other people) turned to regard the Mohican-haired, leather-jacketed punk rocker who was now striding purposefully towards me. I noted the safety pins in his ears, the tattoos on his face, the chains on his combat trousers, his terrifyingly large Doc Marten boots, and I'd judged him and found him guilty before he said a single word. Obviously he was going to beat me up and steal my wallet!

Actually, he was a past pupil (not in uniform now) who simply wanted to swap a few anecdotes about 'the old days' and tell me with pride how much he was enjoying his new training course to become an electrician. After a few minutes he shook my hand forcefully and, all smiles, went on his way. I will never forget that small but significant meeting and the lesson it taught me.

> **TIP:**
> Explore visual symbols. Ask students to interpret the possible meanings of various symbols (religious, scientific, heraldic), and to create new ones for themselves.

Application

- Ask students to bring in books that they have read (or are at least familiar with). Encourage the rest of the group to discuss a book's cover and decide what it's about and whether or not they would want to read it. Include non-fiction books. Useful discussion can follow on how cover design is the clever and sophisticated art of creating particular impressions in the minds of potential readers.

- Discuss the personality behind the face. Use pictures of faces of unknown people. Discuss what kind of people they might be. Highlight assumptions and inferences, elicit justifications of any prejudice (which comes from the Latin *pre judicium*, 'judging before [the fact]'). What do you make of the faces below?

Concept

The eyes have it

The eyes are very expressive – or, more accurately, the eyes and surrounding facial muscles are very expressive. When we interact with another person, a great deal is communicated not just by the voice, but by body posture and facial expression, including the cast of the eyes. Sometimes these signals are contradictory: we may say one thing but our 'non verbals' tell another story. Some time ago a mutual acquaintance joined a friend and myself for a drink. After the acquaintance left, my friend said 'He smiles a lot doesn't he? But, did you notice, not with his eyes...'

Being aware of what someone's eyes might be telling us is a useful aspect of EI.

Application

- Ask students to decide which emotions are being communicated by the sets of eyes below.
- Match up the pairs of eyes with the accompanying faces. Which emotions are being expressed?
- Ask students to draw their own 'circle faces' expressing a greater range of emotions.
- Look at pictures of faces from magazines and comics. Ask students to infer the emotions being expressed. Which visual clues influenced their decisions?

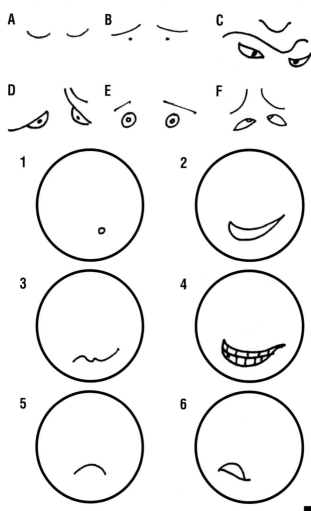

Concept

Body language

When most people hear the phrase 'body language' they think of the way body posture communicates messages that may or may not fit with what that person is saying. There are many books on this subject and the better ones, I think, make the useful point that reading body language is not an exact science. Folded arms might be a defensive reaction, or might indicate that the person is cold, or simply feels more comfortable in that position.

Encouraging students to be more aware of their own and others' body posture is a useful aspect of EI. We have already seen how, for instance, noticing that your shoulders are hunched or tensed and then dropping them aids relaxation. By the same token, if you are talking with someone who is nervous, by adopting their posture initially and then gradually shifting to a more open and relaxed posture yourself, you are offering a non-verbal prompt for that person to follow your lead. In the field of Neuro-Linguistic Programming (NLP) this technique is called 'mirroring and pacing'. You'll find some useful NLP books listed in the References section if you want to learn more.

The kind of body language I want to focus on here, however, refers to the huge diversity of similes and metaphors pertaining to the body. Our language abounds with such references such as 'Head and shoulders above the rest', 'Keeping your ear to the ground' and 'He has a nose for a good deal'. Exploring these similes and metaphors enriches our ability to communicate and develops our insight into the way thoughts, feelings and physical behaviours are connected.

Application

- Ask students to compile a list of similes, metaphors, proverbs, phrases and sayings that refer to the body (you may feel the need to mention at this point that certain examples will not be appropriate!). Link such sayings with the emotions they suggest. For example…
    - She walks around with her nose in the air – arrogance, pride, aloofness.
    - He really put his foot in it – social clumsiness, lack of sensitivity.
    - She's so two-faced! – untrustworthy, deceitful.
- Adapt such metaphors, or create new ones, to communicate positive ideas.
    - She's always on eye-level with you – talks to you as an equal, doesn't look down on you.
    - He quick-stepped that situation really well – danced elegantly around a possible social difficulty.
    - She was one-faced about it when I asked her – honest and truthful.

He really put his foot in it

We see eye to eye

Concept

Sound affects

'Affect' is another term for emotion. The human voice is incredibly versatile and expressive of our feelings. Not only that, but the reflective and deliberate use of tonal qualities when we speak communicates much more than the mere content of the words themselves (ask any cat or dog owner). The artful use of the voice is a powerful way of managing social situations above and beyond what we say, and can profoundly influence other people's reactions.

There are many elements that combine to produce a human voice and convey its tone, such as volume, tempo and pace. These are the sub-modalities, the parts that make up the whole. One benefit of noticing these more deliberately is to spot when, for instance, someone's voice says one thing but their eyes or facial expression or body position sends a different signal.

In working with the voice as linked with the emotions, it's worth bearing in mind the following sub-modalities (aspects of sound):

- Volume – loud–quiet
- Tone – bass–treble
- Pitch – high–low
- Tempo – fast–slow
- Distance – close–far
- Rhythm
- Location

An awareness of these sub-modalities helps us to listen out for subtexts and clues in other people's and our own voices. It develops our mental ability to notice thoughts in greater (sensory) detail.

Application

■ Watch video clips with your students, encouraging them to pay particular attention to the way the characters use their voices to reflect their feelings. It is also interesting to watch some clips with the volume turned off and infer emotions from facial expression and body posture.

■ Listen to audio clips from films and pick out the sub-modalities of the characters' voices.

■ Set up some 'what if' situations (which the students may want to improvise through role play) and discuss the tonal qualities of people's voices in those situations.

   – What if you had been given, and kept, £10 extra in your change at a shop and you were now telling your friends about it?

   – What if you had been given a birthday present from family or a close friend that you really didn't like – how would you sound as you opened it in front of them?

   – What if you'd been accused of doing something wrong when, in fact, you were innocent?

■ Listen to examples of stirring or inspiring speaking. Which qualities of the speaker's voice add to the power of what he or she is saying?

■ Ask your students to be particularly aware of how they use their voices in the situations they'll encounter in the following days.

■ Listen to musical instruments one at a time. Pick out the sub-modalities of the sounds they make. If the sounds were feelings, which emotions would they be?

Concept

Sensory journey

Because our feelings and physical reactions are so deeply influenced by what and how we think, developing the deliberate use of the imagination allows us to manage our feelings more powerfully. An important idea in education is that of 'metacognition' – thinking about the thinking we do. A precursor to effective metacognition is noticing what's going on in our heads in the first place.

We often use the phrases 'make up your mind' and 'change your mind' rather casually. But actually these are mental skills that we can employ more effectively as our metacognitive abilities grow. 'Think before you act' is not a universal law, but it remains a useful rule of thumb in many situations. The techniques on the opposite page develop metacognition across the range of sensory modalities.

Application

- Say to your students 'Imagine there is a person waiting outside to speak to us.' Now use the flip of a coin to answer your group's yes–no questions about this imaginary character (heads = yes, tails = no). So, if the first question is 'Is this person female?' and the answer is yes, then all the students who initially imagined a male figure outside the room now have to change their minds deliberately. Subsequent yes–no answers mean that students must refresh and refine their mental impression, detail by detail, as they construct an increasingly rich scenario.

- Play some instrumental music. Say to your group 'Pretend this music is a landscape. As it plays, write down the kind of landscape you imagine.' This cross-matching of sensory impressions is one aspect of *synaesthesia* (see also p60). You can cross-match any of the senses in this way. Show the students a colour and ask them to imagine it is a flavour; or use a musical instrument to make a sound and ask about the texture of the sound. For further ideas on this, see my book *100 Ideas for Teaching Creativity*.

- Develop a sensory visualization. Set the scene: 'You are walking past a petrol station and suddenly inhale a whiff of petrol fumes. Describe that smell as you would to somebody who has never smelled petrol before. Later, just as you reach a bus shelter, there is a sudden heavy downpour. Describe the sound of the rain on the perspex roof of the shelter' – encourage the students to develop their descriptions beyond the obvious such as pitter-patter.

Concept

Self-estimating

The writer P. G. Wodehouse was once asked if he read the reviews of his books: he replied 'No, but I do weigh them.' He understood that to feel uplifted by a good review made him as much a 'victim' of someone else's opinion as feeling crushed by another critic's bad review. At least a good weight of reviews meant that his work had caused a stir…

Of course we enjoy getting sincere praise. It's also often the case that we base our sense of self-esteem on what other people say about us, whereas self-esteem truly means how we estimate ourselves. Low self-esteem can be very inhibiting and is linked to the idea of the 'triangle of failure'…

Imagine a triangle with 'failure of capability' at the top. At the other two points we find 'failure of nerve' and 'failure of imagination'. Some motivational gurus assert that we all have the potential to be brilliant at everything. Whether this is true or not, people's abilities can be held back by a fear of failure or simply by not imagining success powerfully enough. Addressing these issues raises self-esteem and allows capabilities to flourish.

It is wisely said that an angry man lives in an angry world. The modern equivalent of this idea is that 'perception is projection'. We don't see reality as it is, but as we are – we filter experience through a complex net of beliefs, values and attitudes. Recognizing this is an important leap in EI; keeping our thinking flexible and appreciating other people's viewpoints is another.

Application

- Positive Self Review. Sit quietly (use the chilling out techniques you have learned, see chapter 2) and think back to times when you have done something with confidence. This might be something simple and mundane, but as you remember it, feel the sense of confidence you experienced at the time. Do the same for any incidents that brought out your 'noble qualities' such as kindness, generosity and tolerance. These events are not about what other people said or did but about how you reacted. Make a note of these memories. Begin to cultivate these qualities deliberately now in your day-to-day life.

- Dare to do something that takes you a step outside your 'comfort zone'. If you are standing at a supermarket checkout, exchange pleasantries with the cashier or the next customer in line. Dare to be positive. Dare to be a little more confident.

- If someone expresses a negative opinion about you, consider that it may be more to do with their 'baggage' than with you. Avoid 'mind reading' other people – catch yourself in the act of thinking that other people are criticizing you. What evidence do you have? If there is any, is any of it valid? If it is (and make sure you've reached a balanced judgement) what will you now do to change these people's minds?

- Distinguish between attainment and achievement. Consider the idea that attainment is someone else's assessment of you, but that achievement comes from within. If I write a book and no-one wants to publish it, my achievement is to have written that book. No-one can deny that, diminish it or take it away from me.

Concept

Perceptual filtering

There is an ancient story about a hermit who lived on a hill. A town lay in the valley to the East, and another town lay in a similar valley to the West. One morning the hermit sat on his front porch and watched a young man labouring up the slope towards him from the eastern valley. When he arrived, hot and thirsty from his climb, the hermit offered him refreshment and they fell into conversation.

The young man explained that he was seeking new opportunities in the town to the West. 'I have loved my home,' he went on. 'The people are so friendly, but it's time to move on. Do you know what the people in West Town are like?' 'I think,' said the hermit, 'that you'll find them to be just the same.' The young traveller went on his way.

A week later, the hermit noticed another traveller in the distance, this time approaching from the West. The hermit offered refreshment and the two sat and chatted.

'I'm going to seek my fortune in East Town,' this young man explained. 'I'm fed up with the West Valley people. They are so unfriendly and unhelpful… Do you know East Town?' he asked. 'What are the people like there?'

To which the hermit replied, 'I think you will find them to be just the same.'

Application

Use the picture below or one similar. Say 'Imagine you can step into this picture. Stand on the pavement. What do you notice? What are your thoughts and feelings?' The students visualize this and report their impressions. On a subsequent occasion, ask the students to step into the picture as elderly people, muggers, town planners, young women coming home from a club, local shopkeepers, etc. Keep changing the students' viewpoint.

Concept

Three perceptual positions (3PP)

This is a simple, flexible and effective technique for encouraging students to accept someone else's viewpoint. The three perceptual positions are...

1. One's own viewpoint on a given topic or issue

2. An opposing viewpoint

3. The neutral observer

This technique can serve to break what is often a habit of looking at the world and reacting to experiences in the same way.

Our perceptions are filtered by our emotional state. If we actively seek to change the way we 'look' at the world, we can then become more flexible in the way we respond emotionally. It might help to realize that the word 'responsibility' can mean 'response-ability', the ability we have to respond flexibly and deliberately.

TIP:
A powerful question to ask if you have to intervene in a dispute is 'How do you think (the other person) feels?'.

Application

- Set up three chairs, two facing each other with the third forming the third point of an equilateral triangle. Decide on the issue to be explored beforehand; three students then take up the three perceptual positions. It helps initially if students 1 and 2 actually hold those opposing viewpoints. The student in position 3 must simply observe and note ideas without taking sides.
- Student 1 now puts forward her viewpoint; then student 2 puts his. They may speak for a certain length of time and read from a prepared script. Student 3 sums up each viewpoint afterwards and comments are invited from the rest of the class. No decision need be taken about who is 'right' or has the stronger argument.
- Develop the technique by changing the positions of students 1 and 2 before the exchange of views begins, thereby creating the opportunity to see things from the opposing side. Subsequently, the students involved in the activity move through positions 1, 2 and 3 so they all experience all viewpoints. Encourage discussion about how the process felt.

Concept

Exploring values

After several thousand years, philosophers still debate whether morality is absolute (God-given or genetic) – are we born with a sense of right and wrong, or do we learn it through childhood? Whatever the answer, as we grow older we can explore these concepts more and more powerfully, drawing on our experiences and our developing intellectual abilities.

Our notion of 'values' comes from the Latin *valere*, meaning to be worth, be strong. This is the same root that gives rise to 'valuable' (as in precious) and also 'valour' (courage in adversity). The implication here is that our values are not, and should not be, fickle, changing as the wind blows, but remain firm even in adverse circumstances. In the Northern mythological tradition the word 'troth' was a firm promise, a solid bond of trust (more generally applied than in our modern particular sense of 'bethrothal'). For the Norse peoples, troth-breaking was one of the greatest and most serious of crimes.

Application

'What if' dilemmas

Pose a difficult situation to your group and ask your students what they would do in the circumstances. Start with absurd, whimsical or wacky scenarios and progress towards more searching 'real life' situations. So, for example…

- If you could be any fictional character (from film, TV or a book) for a day, who would you be and why?
- Would you eat a bowl of bugs for £500? – increase the amount of money progressively.
- If you had a 50 per cent chance of winning a bet (say the flip of a coin) and would pick up ten times what you gambled, what proportion of your fortune would you risk? How did you reach your decision?
- What if you could trade the length of your life for greater success? The more years you gave, the more successful you could be now. How much would you give?

See Gregory Stock's *The Book of Questions* for many more fine examples.

Decision alley

1. Decide with your class on a controversial issue to explore.

2. Split the class into three groups: one group for the issue or proposal (A); one group arguing against (B); and one group who are undecided or deliberately neutral (C).

3. Ask each student in groups A and B to write out a brief statement in support of their viewpoint.

4. With groups A and B forming two lines facing one another, ask the students from group C to walk slowly between the lines while the A and B students quietly reiterate their statements.

5. Ask the C students if they have made up their minds now, and why.

6. Switch the groups' positions with the same or different issues.

Concept

Modify the memory

When we remember things that have happened to us we draw upon our resource of memory and represent the experience in our imagination. Now let's use 'resource' as a verb – we 're-source', go back again to the source of our ability to think. And we 're-present', we present once more how we interpreted the original experience.

These are powerful ideas because they allow us to realize that we do not need passively to remember things in the same way that we have always remembered them. Rather, we can proactively modify our memories to serve our purposes more usefully. I once worked with a man who, in talking about his low self-esteem always mentioned a particularly intimidating teacher he'd had in junior school. And every time my client talked of this teacher he would look up and see him looming over. I said 'Why do you always put him up there, looking down on you?' 'That's how I remember him,' my client said. 'Then remember him differently now,' I suggested. And we began to work on shifting my client's perspective so that the teacher was below and smaller instead of being above and bigger. After a few minutes of rehearsing this, my client could think of his old teacher in this new way and not feel so intimidated.

For much more information on very elegant techniques for working in this way see *Monsters and Magical Sticks* by Steven Heller and Terry Steele.

Application

- Begin to notice how you remember past experiences. If the memory is pleasant you can enhance the way you bring it back to mind. If you are remembering in colour, make the colours brighter. If you hear sounds and voices, make them more distinct. Actively notice the good feelings attached to the memory and 'turn them up' like turning up colour and brightness and volume on a TV.

- If the memory is unpleasant, deliberately change the way you imagine it. Make intimidating people smaller. Give them cartoon-character voices. Put them in ridiculous positions. If you feel angry as you remember, use the anger to help yourself feel better – I must confess that when I think of one unpleasant incident that happened to me I imagine myself picking up the other person involved and hurling him far into the sky as Superman would. I hear my 'enemy' land with a satisfying splat a long way away.

- Imagine yourself floating above any negative experience in which you were involved. Be a big brother or sister to yourself: give yourself advice on how best to deal with the situation. Intend that similar wisdom will come to you if ever you are involved in any similar situation.

Concept

Mediating

To mediate comes from the Latin root for *middle* and means to find common ground between extremes or, in terms of one's own attitude, to find the middle way. This is an idea that lies, for instance, at the heart of the Buddha's teachings with regard to a person's conduct towards others, rooted in spiritual awareness and a sense of respect. These values surely form the core of all religious teachings.

However, the will to walk the middle way, or to help others find that route, can be applied at any level. As responsible adults in charge of young people we are often required to intervene to prevent or defuse disagreements and disputes among our students, helping them to moderate their reactions, find a compromise and come to a settlement – as we must in our personal lives, based on the recognition that 'No one is an island' (*John Donne*).

TIP:
Make students aware of keywords in the vocabulary of mediation, such as 'compromise' – a mutual promise to abide by an agreement; 'concession' – to give up something for the greater common good; 'respect' – to look back or look again on, in order to gain a new viewpoint.

Application

Mediation line

This is a line with a number scale of 1–6 above. Offer students statements and ask them to estimate how far they agree. Increasingly demand reasons and justifications for their assessment. So…

- The richer you are the greater the percentage of your income you should pay in tax.
- Children should be seen and not heard.
- Things aren't what they used to be.
- Everybody should do at least one charitable thing each day.

Establish immediately that emotional or disrespectful responses aren't usually very persuasive. Often the most powerful influence of opinion comes from a quietly argued and well-reasoned case.

Finding common ground

Draw a mediation line and write the topic at issue above it. Establish two opposing viewpoints. Mark a point halfway along the line. This is the common ground where settlement can be reached. Ask students to align themselves with one viewpoint or the other. The task now is for each group in turn to suggest a way forward, step by step, towards compromise.

Concept

Anchoring

When I was a young boy in primary school I remember that when my teacher intended to give the class a 'spot test', he would always position himself in front of his desk, which stood to one side of the blackboard. Over time, just to see him moving into that position filled me (and most of the rest of us) with dread, because we just knew that another test was on its way.

An anchor is a link that is created between a particular response you want to elicit in yourself and/or others, and something you have under your direct conscious control. Anchors can be positive or – as in the anecdote above – not so positive. Also, my teacher never realized the effect that his standing in front of the desk was having on the class. He was developing the anchor (standing in front of desk = imminent test) inadvertently.

Anchoring is a powerful and flexible technique often used in NLP and other areas of communication and interaction. It can be applied simply and effectively.

Anchoring effects are cumulative. The link is at first made consciously, but as the habit develops, it becomes more of an automatic reflex.

Application

Spatial anchoring

Designate particular areas in your room where you expect certain behaviour to occur. Spatial anchors can be overt, as in the use of a story corner, where the students come to learn that being there means good sitting and listening, coupled with the pleasant anticipation of the story about to be told. Or you can develop spatial anchors 'subliminally'. Here you designate certain spots where you will stand to elicit different responses from the class. Don't mention you're doing this to the students; the association will be formed subconsciously in their minds. So you may pick a spot where you stand to introduce new ideas, or a spot where you always stand when you expect (and will praise) questioning and discussion from the group. Try a 'discipline spot'. Stand there each time you need to enforce sanctions or remind students about their behaviour. Establish one anchor spot at a time and always be absolutely consistent about where you stand.

Kinesthetic anchor for self-confidence

You can teach this application to students. Each time a student does something well (by her own reckoning or that of others) she rubs her thumb and little finger together – right-handed students use the left hand, and vice versa. Remind the student as many times as needed to develop the habit. A link is thus created – literally a neural pathway in the brain – that finger-rub = something well done. Subsequently, if the student needs a confidence boost, she can do the same finger-rub to elicit those positive feelings.

Concept

Points of praise

Two of the most powerful motivators in developing students' confidence and willingness to learn are quick feedback and sincere praise. When you ask a student to do a particular behaviour such as concentrating, questioning, listening, speculating, as the student carries out that task, verify it for him – let him know you've noticed that he's doing what you've asked him to do. Because you've confirmed it's the right behaviour, any praise you give must, logically, be sincere.

This is an obvious strategy which good teachers use anyway. However it must be used artfully. I once witnessed a teacher say to a misbehaving pupil, 'Oh Tyler, I'm so pleased that you stopped hitting Conner when I asked you to.' There was no condemnation of Tyler's aggression, just praise that it had stopped! (And it didn't seem like sincere praise either, just relief that another crisis had been averted.)

Self-esteem really means 'how we estimate ourselves'. Sadly many people's sense of self-esteem is dependent upon the judgements of others. Encouraging independence of judgement, modesty and sincere praise of others' efforts are all effective in building self-esteem.

> **TIP:**
> Be firm in eliciting the behaviour you want from students. Say 'Sit down now please' as a command rather than as a question 'Shall we sit down now please?' which smacks of desperation and allows children to think 'No, we won't'. Avoid the old chestnut, 'I'm waiting…' The students already know this – and will keep you waiting if they're feeling rebellious.

Application

- Encourage students to be sincere in their praise of each other. Take the lead of course in praising work well done, but you can increasingly invite students to appreciate their classmates' endeavours. This is especially necessary, I feel, in an education system that is so competitive and the product of a win or lose mentality.
- Employ the 'three points of praise and one point of improvement' technique when reviewing students' work. There is psychological significance in the number three. One point of praise might be attributed to luck, two points of praise to coincidence – but when the teacher has noticed a third thing done well, the weight of evidence shifts and the student can feel that the praise is sincere, that he really has done something well. In many primary schools the techniques is called 'three stars and a wish'; however, I think a wish is a passive thing open to the fickleness of fortune. I prefer to use the word 'intention'.

Healthy language

Concept

Language and perception

Earlier in the book I mentioned the idea that we see the world not as it is, but as we are (see Perceptual filtering, p42). We can now adapt that slightly to 'we say the world not as it is, but as we are'. Our words have their roots in our beliefs and attitudes. Our perceptions both conscious and subconscious are revealed in the language we use to frame them.

Consider the sentence 'This problem is really hard'. Notice the connotations of the word 'hard'. Stone is hard; steel is hard. When we say that something is hard we evoke or imply the network of associations we have built up over time with that idea. The problem might of course be difficult, but how differently we can feel about it if we say 'This problem is intriguing' or 'That idea makes me ask lots of questions'.

> I once had a conversation with a teacher who was giving up smoking. She said 'It's like that legend of the man who rolls the boulder uphill forever as a punishment!'. I suggested she imagine that she could now tilt the whole landscape so that the boulder rolled to the top of the hill. She laughed, but said she'd give that a try. A few days later she'd quit smoking effortlessly.

Application

- Watch your language. A teacher once asked me how I dealt with writer's block. I told her, and the class, that I put a doorway in it and walked through. The children (eight to nine year olds) then told me you could float over it in a hot air balloon, or use a jetpack or a trampoline, or get a team of elephants to drag it out of the way… Yes, this is only playing with words – but we say the world not as it is, but as we are. Furthermore, each idea suggests a different strategy for dealing with the situation. Continuing with such creative word- and metaphor-play might well make those strategies explicit (see also my book *100 Ideas for Teaching Creativity*).

- Dig to the roots. Exploring the etymology of language develops greater sensitivity to meanings and greater discernment in word use. 'Problem' for instance comes from the Greek meaning 'to throw forwards'. Playing with this notion can change one's perception of it helpfully. I throw a ball forwards in play, or as part of a game that I engage with for the challenge. Similarly, the word 'lesson' has links with 'legend', from the Latin 'to gather, select, read' and is akin to the Greek *logos* meaning 'speech, word, reason'. A legend of course is also an exciting and instructive story.

- Help students to recognize cognitive distortions in their language (see p9 and p15). This includes the use of negative and unhelpful superlatives such as 'I'll **never** be able to do this!', 'I **always** have trouble with reading', '**Everyone**'s better than me!'.

Concept

Get a better metaphor

All language is representational. The word is not the thing. Or, to put it another way, the menu is not the meal. When we use language we are not dealing with reality but with structures of thought, beliefs and perceptions. Talking for instance about 'the run up to Christmas' casts it in a certain light. Why a 'run up'? Why don't we say 'The leisurely stroll up to Christmas'? We easily could, and that might take some of the stress out of it! Consider too the associations of the word 'stress' – many materials shatter under too much stress.

Linguists call a verb (describing a process) that becomes a noun a nominalization. Many abstract nouns are nominalizations. The first point to note is that while nominalizations may make perfect grammatical sense they beg many questions. So for example, 'The foundation of every state is the education of its youth' (Diogenes). Here 'education' is used as a noun, a label. But notice what's missing: who is being educated by whom?; what does it consist of?; how do we know if it is happening?; who ultimately decides when it is successful?.

Asking for further, detailed information can help us to get more of a handle on nominalizations. Make students aware of this linguistic illusion, especially when they apply it unhelpfully to themselves. I came across a student who told me he was 'a real loser'. I asked him what did he mean by 'real', in what sense precisely was he 'losing', how exactly was he measuring this losing process?

Application

- Forge metaphorical links using feelings. Choose, say, the weather as a theme. Make a list of pleasant and unpleasant feelings and match them with aspects of the weather. Many examples already exist in our language. We talk about somebody having a sunny disposition, or storming out of the room or having a thunderous look. Because the weather is a series of ongoing processes, once the comparison has been made, we can use it to change the feeling. Using visualization, how can we now 'change the weather' that gave somebody a thunderous expression?

- Combine the recognition of unhelpful nominalizations with metaphors. Take a playful approach, for example:

    Teacher: So, if 'losing' were an animal, which animal would it be?

    Student: Um, a cat...

    Teacher: Because?

    Student: A scaredy cat hiding away, because 'losing' makes you ashamed and want to hide.

    Teacher: Let's change the animal in a helpful way. Maybe it could still be a cat, but now –

    Student: Yeah, a lion. Because he's strong and proud, and that's how you can be if you lose. It's nothing to be ashamed of. It helps you to deal with things as you learn to do it better...

You may need to guide and suggest to help the student create the more helpful metaphor or nominalization.

Concept

Synaesthesia – a union of sensations

The definition of synaesthesia according to Wikipedia, the online free encyclopedia, is 'a neurological condition in which two or more bodily senses are coupled', although more generally it also means a cross-matching of sensory impressions during perception, which can take place in the imagination on a metaphorical level. 'Neurological synaesthetes' might perceive sounds as having colours, for example, or words (read or spoken) as having flavours. This intriguing phenomenon is increasingly being regarded as a powerful way of making sense of the world (see http://en.wikipedia.org/wiki/Synaesthesia).

For further synaesthesia activities, see *Pocket PAL: Boys and Writing*.

> **TIP:**
> The language of wine-tasting is rich with multisensory references. Words such as austere, big, earthy, green, high notes, undertones, are all wine-tasting terms. An internet search will reveal many more. Encourage students to describe odours and flavours in this more expansive way.

Application

- Develop students' sensory acuity by introducing them to 'metaphorical synaesthesia'. Show your group a colour and say 'If this were a sound, what would it sound like?'. Or sound a musical instrument such as a rattle and say 'If this were a flavour, what would it taste like?'.

- Teach students the following technique for dealing with unhelpful/unpleasant feelings. As the teacher/mentor, you don't need to know what the feeling is. Begin by saying 'If this feeling you'd like to change had a colour, what would it be?'.

- Once the student has given a colour, go through the senses. What shape is the feeling? How heavy is it? How warm? Give it a smell – what does it smell like? Tap it, what sound does it make? End by saying 'And if it was located somewhere inside you, where would that be?'.

- When the feeling has been defined in this way, quickly have the student change every aspect of it; change the colour, weight, sound, and so on. Then tell the student to relocate the feeling in his body. When he's done that, have him pretend to take it in his hand and throw it away.

- Now divert the student's attention – 'What's that outside? Oh, just a bird.' And then ask him how he feels. The unpleasant emotion will most likely have faded.

Concept

Dear diary

A diary is most usually a personal account of one's own experiences – the things that have happened to us, the ups and downs of life; a record of the details of events. More helpfully it can be used to express how we feel. Often a person's most powerful and insightful writing occurs when she is in the 'flow of composition', not struggling to think of what to say or which words to use, but simply letting the ideas pour out on to the page.

This process occurs when one is in a state of 'relaxed alertness', the so-called *alpha state* when we are aware of the outflow of thoughts from the subconscious mind and can refine them without struggle as we frame them in words. For more details of the alpha state see, for instance, Guy Claxton's *Hare Brain, Tortoise Mind.*

Because writing a diary is a quiet and private act where there is no pressure to compete, succeed or achieve, encouraging it is an effective way of anchoring (see p52) and developing the alpha state. Diary-keeping can also be used in other ways in the field of EI...

Application

Emotions diary

Encourage students to keep an emotions diary, not focusing particularly on external events but rather on the interplay of one's emotions. The simple act of expressing feelings can help to moderate them if they are negative and remember positive feelings when the diary is reread. Some students may feel more at ease using drawings, rather than words, to express their emotions.

Achievements diary

Record only those things you feel pleased about and proud of, even down to the smallest act of kindness, politeness or generosity.

Positive feelings diary

Similarly, consider a positive feelings diary, with reasons attached – 'Today I felt really happy because…'

Another person's diary

Write in the first person from someone else's perspective. This is especially powerful if you yourself were involved in that person's experiences (see also Perceptual filtering, p42).

Parallel diary

This is a double account, of things as they actually happened and the way you would have liked things to happen. The emphasis here is not on wishful thinking, but on reflection so that you are better prepared should similar circumstances arise in the future.

Future diary

Anticipate positive outcomes. Imagine future success and achievement. Write as though it had already happened. Use the writing process as an anchor (see p52) to connect to good feelings. Also, allow yourself to write about what you did to get to that point – for instance, explore strategies that led, or will lead, to your success.

Concept

Lifelines

We usually think of our lives in a linear way, like a story. We have a beginning, middle and an end. The term 'life story' epitomizes this perception. Life 'lines' viewed like this reflects cultural biases and the dominance of the left hemisphere of the neocortex, the part of the brain that is largely responsible for logical-sequential thinking and language.

If you are interested in this concept, I recommend Tad James's excellent book *Time Line Therapy and the Basis of Personality*.

Thinking of a life as a line is not the only way it can be imagined. Even this quite limiting view, however, can be utilized...

Application

- Draw your lifeline up to the present. Give it a time scale and mark significant times such as achievements, successes and good times.
- Project your lifeline into the future. Mark potential and intended successes. Write letters to your future self, asking for tips and advice. This might sound odd, but actually it works very well based on the principle that we 'know more than we think we know'
- Turn the line into a tree. Create a 'possibility tree' (see also p73). Take a large sheet of paper. Draw a line to indicate the recent past. Grow branches out from it to indicate options and choices you might make. Select a branch and grow further branches out from that. Annotate the branches to indicate what these choices might lead to. What would you need to do to reach that point? What might stop you? How can you overcome that?

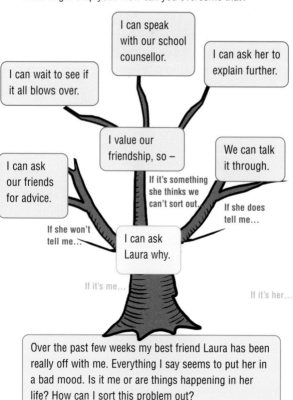

I can speak with our school counsellor.

I can ask her to explain further.

I can wait to see if it all blows over.

I value our friendship, so –

We can talk it through.

I can ask our friends for advice.

If it's something she thinks we can't sort out.

If she does tell me...

If she won't tell me...

I can ask Laura why.

If it's me...

If it's her...

Over the past few weeks my best friend Laura has been really off with me. Everything I say seems to put her in a bad mood. Is it me or are things happening in her life? How can I sort this problem out?

Concept

Futurescopes

Read any tabloid or magazine horoscope and notice the language. It tends to be very generalized and vague (look out too for nominalizations – see p58). Its influence lies in the human tendency to contextualize. We like to know more: we feel the urge to see the bigger picture in order to make decisions about future actions. We weave these threads of information into the fabric of our greater understanding.

Horoscope language (and whether or not there is any truth or reality behind horoscopes is not the point) can be exploited to help develop EI.

1. consider your needs and the environment.
2. partnerships are likely.
3. it's time for a parting or separation.
4. be sensitive to signals and coincidence.
5. be strong and determined now.
6. you are about to break into new areas.
7. things happen to limit you.
8. you move into a fertile environment.
9. look to your defences.
10. to protect now will prevent difficulty later.
11. possessions change their significance.
12. joy is coming soon in new ways.
13. openings lie ahead.
14. soon you will reap the harvest of your efforts.
15. be prepared to work for whatever you want.
16. this is a time of new growth.
17. move on and see obstacles removed.
18. don't fight, just go along with circumstances.
19. everything is about to suffer disturbance.
20. important messages are imminent.
21. a deliberate change of direction brings benefits.
22. be patient, you stand on a threshold.
23. around lies the solution to a problem.
24. recognize the usefulness of standing still.
25. look at the whole thing again to see anew.
26. knowledge comes now from what was unknown.

Application

■ Write the horoscope 'statements' (opposite) on scraps of paper. Ask students to choose one or two at random and then use them to make positive predictions about what might happen soon.

■ Use a horoscope idea with the If-Then game. This activity explores themes, contexts and relationships, and makes useful cause-effect links. So **if** everything is about to suffer a disturbance, **then** that might mean (for example) I fall out with my friend. **If** I am going to fall out with my friend, **then** I can do these things to stop it – A/B/C… **If** I fall out with my friend anyway, **then** this is what I could do to mend matters – D/E/F…

■ Use horoscope language with the Maybe Hand game (see p72). Important messages are imminent – maybe this means A, B, C, D or E. Speculation like this generates several options to be considered before a decision is made.

■ Identify nominalizations (see p58) in horoscope language and question yourself or others to gather more specific information. 'Knowledge comes now from what was unknown'. Exactly what counts as knowledge? What particular knowledge comes now? How? What precisely is unknown? How does knowledge come from that? How can I best use it?

Concept

Character pie

We are all a complex mix of 'ingredients'; experiences, beliefs, strengths, insecurities, ideas... Character pie is a generic idea that translates into many games and activities for self-exploration.

Acknowledging and exploring the different facets of our emotional make-up can help us towards a better understanding and awareness of our behaviour and feelings.

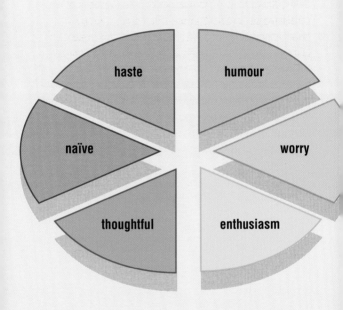

Application

- Ask students to write about themselves as though they were recipes. For instance, 'I am plenty of fresh-picked ideas laced with curiosity, spiced with mischief and generously topped with lots of fun'.
- Use the above game to help students visualize positive changes in themselves. If your anger were chilli powder, how could you improve the dish now?
- Students make a character collage using pictures clipped from magazines, individual words, phrases, pieces of material, small stones, shells, leaves, glitter and so on, to create an abstract and impressionistic view of a person. Begin by 'collaging' fictional characters, famous people and historical figures; then ask students to create a collage of themselves. Students aren't required to reveal any personal details or to explain what the collage means. Its primary value is in the act of expression. Once a collage has been created, that student can make changes to it, representing positive changes she intends to make in herself.
- Box of treasures. Students fill a small box with objects that represent their strengths, achievements and qualities.

Concept

Snapshot

We all know the phrases 'jumping to conclusions', 'making snap judgements' and 'unwarranted assumptions'. All of these boil down to making up one's mind prematurely with insufficient information. In the field of thinking skills, an assumption is a kind of mental 'destination' that we arrive at based more on what we think, rather than what is going on in the outside world. When we assume something, we usually haven't done a thorough reality check.

Inferring, or concluding, is slightly more reliable. Here we make judgements about a pattern based on what has happened before. As I walk down the High Street I notice that the first five red-headed people I see look miserable. I infer from this that the next red-headed person I see is likely to be miserable. Actually this may or may not be true. Such an inference is neither logical nor scientific. Furthermore, although those five red-headed people looked unhappy *to me*, maybe in fact they were not. Or, even if they were, it would probably have been for five entirely different reasons. Or maybe 'unhappy' is too vague an idea to apply to any of them…

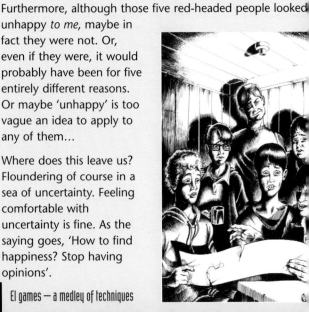

Where does this leave us? Floundering of course in a sea of uncertainty. Feeling comfortable with uncertainty is fine. As the saying goes, 'How to find happiness? Stop having opinions'.

> Abraham Lincoln once said that 'People are as happy as they make up their minds to be'. If we hold on to the belief that unpleasant, unfortunate circumstances inevitably mean that someone must necessarily be downtrodden and unhappy, then that person remains a passive victim of 'fate'. Improving one's lot in life begins within. Inner change brings personal power.

Application

Context sentences

These are sentences that offer some information but beg many questions. Use them to highlight how easy it is to speculate, assume and infer. Use in conjunction with the 'Maybe Hand' (see p72). Some examples are…

- She gasped and fell to the floor. He walked to the window and smiled.
- Glass shattered nearby – it couldn't be true!
- The child closed his book and folded his arms. 'That's not the kind of behaviour I expect from you,' his teacher said.

Bin bags

Put (clean!) packaging from household items into a plastic bin bag and ask students to come to conclusions about the families in question.

Hypothesis game

Offer students some scraps of information and ask them to create a scenario to account for it. For instance…

- The vase lay smashed on the lounge carpet.
- Nearby lay a framed picture.
- The cat was hiding underneath the kitchen table.
- Jeff, ten years old, ran upstairs to his room.
- Diane, Jeff's sister, hurriedly telephoned her friend.
- Jeff's Mum walked into the lounge. She was in tears.

Every picture tells a story – or two or three…

Use pictures from newspapers, magazines and 'screen grabs' from movies (if you have the technology) and ask students to suggest what might be happening and what might happen next. A drawing, such as the one opposite, can prompt much discussion.

Concept

The Maybe Hand and many endings

In many books on learning, you'll encounter the theory that children learn more willingly and effectively when they feel comfortable with uncertainty and ambiguity. The need to know the right answer right now (on which a great deal of schooling is still based) can so easily give rise to an over-reliance on 'facts' delivered by authority figures, and anxiety in the students (and their teachers?) if those facts can't be recalled at will. Such a need to be sure of facts can also create a fear of being wrong and a reluctance to explore, investigate and remain undecided until enough information has been gathered.

The same things are no less true in the field of EI. The art of wondering is based upon speculation and exploring possibilities. While this happens we hold back from making judgements and investing energy in redundant emotional reactions.

Application

The Maybe Hand. Offer students a situation and ask them to come up with five possible explanations. So, for example, I'm driving along the motorway and a black BMW cuts me up and zooms away on the slip road. Why?

- Maybe because all BMW drivers are lunatics! (A friend of mine believes this and becomes incensed at the very mention of 'BMW', see cognitive distortions on p14).
- Maybe that particular driver is a thoughtless risk taker.
- Maybe he's an undercover police offer on an important case.
- Maybe he's a businessman who's late for an important meeting.
- Maybe his wife has taken ill and been rushed to hospital, and he's hurrying to be with her.

Any or none of these possibilities could be true. How will we ever know? The point is that by remaining undecided on the matter, or by retaining the power to choose, we have more control over our emotional responses. How different our feelings will be if we choose to think that he's a loyal husband rushing to his poorly wife's bedside.

With younger children, get them to draw around their own hands, write or draw the scenario in the middle and jot down their maybes in the finger spaces.

Possibility or decision trees (see also p65). This is an extension of the above idea, where any 'maybe' throws up further possibilities for action. For instance, suppose I inherited £100,000. What could I do with it? Maybe I'll spend it… Now grow some further branches to explore possible outcomes or consequences.

Concept

El Monopoly...

Adapting the format of existing board games not only gives students an opportunity for some creative thinking, but when they then play those games they rehearse in a valuable way the kinds of responses that might be useful to them in 'the real world'.

Games can create a microcosm of the real world, a small-scale arena where rules, roles, rights and responsibilities can be rehearsed under controlled conditions. Although some games rely heavily on luck (as, indeed, do some real life situations) there is more often an element of skill involved which depends upon a range of considered responses. Games also act as 'playgrounds' – learning zones – for the way situations might evolve based on our responses.

TIP:
You can enrich games by embedding them in a story. Take for instance *Cinderella*. The players are characters from the tale and situations are taken or derive from the story. For older students use a text they're studying – *Lord of the Flies* would be interesting!

Application

El Monopoly

Use the Monopoly® board format but invent a hypothetical town. Each player assumes a role – these may be written out beforehand and chosen at random. So we might have for instance a successful entrepreneur, a penniless vagrant who wants to better himself, a pensioner and a dysfunctional family. As well as Monopoly® money, create 'scenario cards' which involve the players in making decisions that have repercussions for each other. So the entrepreneur has the chance to buy a derelict house in which the vagrant is living. The entrepreneur has permission to develop the land…

Situations are discussed by the students from their perspectives in-role, and as themselves out of role. Possibilities and consequences are explored. Combine the game with other activities in this book, such as possibility trees (see p65), if-then links (see p67), perceptual filtering (see p42) and so on.

El Snakes and Ladders

Use a standard board. Each player has a certain number of tokens they can spend or save as they please. Landing on and zooming up a ladder increases a player's store of tokens. Sliding down a snake lands you in a difficult situation – think of these beforehand and put them on 'chance cards'. If a player is in such a situation the nearest players must decide what to do, whether to help or not, and what kind of help might be offered. Helping out might well cost the helpers some tokens. Do they still do it? If they don't, what might happen if they need help?

Concept

Character profiles

A useful idea is to consider emotional resources as 'treasures' that we gather up during the course of our lives. These largely amount to the 'noble qualities' such as loyalty, kindness, empathy and compassion. Such qualities may be inherent within us (the philosophical jury is still out!), or perhaps we all need to learn these behaviours through the guidance of others and by reflecting upon our own experiences.

Character profiles can be created using a template like the one opposite. You can decide on your own mix of attributes. The 1–6 number line allows a dice to be rolled to give a random 'score' for any of the items on the list. Here are some suggestions for using the profiles...

Application

- Discuss what some of the terms can mean. What does considerate mean? How do you know if you are being clever? Is being calculating a good or bad thing? Are there different sorts of intelligence?
- Use the template to create profiles of characters you meet in stories. Place ticks in the boxes to give each item a score between one and six. How did you decide where to make the marks?
- Discuss differences between apparently similar qualities. Is there a difference between 'intelligent' and 'clever', for example?
- Deliberately change the 'score' of one of the qualities and ask students to consider what other items would now change, and by how much, and why?

	1	2	3	4	5	6
Popular	◯	◯	◯	◯	◯	◯
Generous	◯	◯	◯	◯	◯	◯
Amusing	◯	◯	◯	◯	◯	◯
Clever	◯	◯	◯	◯	◯	◯
Considerate	◯	◯	◯	◯	◯	◯
Calculating	◯	◯	◯	◯	◯	◯
Intelligent	◯	◯	◯	◯	◯	◯

Concept

Desert island

Two key features of being emotionally intelligent are

1. to realize that thoughts determine feelings and actions – each of us is the captain of his or her own ship.

2. actions have consequences. As the saying goes, 'We are defined by our choices', which also define the society in which we live.

Desert island is a simulation game which highlights these ideas. It can be as simple or as sophisticated as you wish, and can focus on any number of EI-related topics.

The purpose of the game is to create from scratch a society that will be viable over time. In a number of ways – which form the focus of discussion – the island is a microcosm of our society, where some of the same problems and dilemmas have to be tackled. The simulation need not involve a great deal of preparation, and can be fitted in to convenient time slots over a period of days or weeks.

Application

- Scenario: a number of your students find themselves marooned on a desert island cut off from the rest of the world. The island itself has plenty of water, trees and wildlife and can sustain the group indefinitely if it is managed correctly. Specify certain items that the castaways have with them such as medical supplies and tools.

- Pose a variety of situations and difficulties to the group. Allow them to discuss the issue and arrive at a decision for action. Reflect on the consequences of the decisions and build them into subsequent scenarios. So, for example…
  - How will the group make decisions? Look at ideas such as democracy, dictatorship, Communism. What are the advantages and disadvantages of each system? Which one do you adopt and why?
  - One member of the group takes more than his share of food, arguing that because he is required to do more physical labour than the rest, he should have more sustenance. What do you think about that claim? What do you decide to do? How did you decide?
  - A sudden storm destroys 20 per cent of the shelters on the island. The unexpectedly homeless want to share your homes. Do you let them?

Concept

Odd-one-in

Odd-one-*out* was a classification exercise that my primary school teacher often used to test our general knowledge. Which item is the odd one out in the following list – rose, daffodil, cabbage, lupin, buttercup?

Did you choose cabbage because it's the only vegetable? Or buttercup because it's the only weed*? My choice is daffodil, because that's the only plant in the list not growing in my garden. This little game has hidden depths if as teachers we don't assume that there is one objectively right answer, and it can be applied usefully to the development of emotional resourcefulness…

101 Ethical Dilemmas by Martin Cohen and *The Philosophy Files* (1 and 2) by Stephen Law offer useful background to some of the ethical dilemmas and philosophical issues that might arise during the simulation.

* Interestingly, in the *Concise Oxford English Dictionary*, a weed is defined as a 'wild plant growing where it is not wanted'. So buttercups for instance are only weeds if I don't want them growing in my lawn. Actually, I think they add a lovely splash of colour to any garden…

Application

Odd-one-out

Play the standard odd-one-out game using terms linked with feelings – affection, confidence, excitement, impatience and sympathy. Now try this one – cynicism, effusiveness, detachment, impulsiveness and sentimentality.

Odd-one-in

Think of other emotions and qualities that could be added to the list – ambition, assertiveness, confidence, exuberance, inspiration, passion, self-assurance, determination and vitality. What might they all have in common?

Yin-Yang

Pick a quality from the list and think of at least one situation where that quality would be an advantage and one where it could well be a disadvantage (or appropriate/inappropriate).

Gradation

Grade emotions and qualities in terms of their strength or intensity (see also Emotion Matrix on p13) – rage, anger, fury, annoyance, aloofness.

Heads and tails

This is an opposites game. If 'happiness' is the heads side of the coin, what would the tails side be?

Analogies

An analogy is a comparison that allows us to explore emotions in more concrete ways. Because we can choose what we compare an emotion with, we can gain greater power in modifying those feelings.

> Rage is to fire as … is to ice?
> Envy is like jealousy because they both…?
> Irritation is to fury as … is to hilarity.

For useful ideas on making analogies see Bellanca and Fogarty, *Teach Them Thinking*.

Concept

Emotion symbols

Symbols acquire greater meaning over time as emotional energy is invested in them. Their usefulness in developing EI is that they act as a kind of shorthand in allowing feelings to be expressed when perhaps the words to do so can't be found and other actions might be inappropriate. Look at the shapes below. What emotions do you think they could represent, and why?

Eleanor Roosevelt once said that no one can make you feel inferior without your own permission. This highlights elegantly and very forcefully that we can be – and can learn to be – more self-determining in the way we handle our own feelings and situations where we are required to deal with others. This section offers some strategies to encourage that journey.

Application

- Ask students to match symbol shapes with feelings. If there is a fair degree of consensus between a symbol and emotion (an arrow matched with aggression for instance) discuss why this might be so. This can lead to deeper insights into the power and value of symbols used in other areas.

- Once an agreed meaning for a symbol has been reached, modify the symbol to express nuances of that emotion. Suggest students change emotion symbols in their imaginations as a visualization (see p24). Link this with the synaesthesia activity (see p60).

- Use emotion symbols with other activities in this book such as diary writing (see p62), control panel (see p88) and metaphors (see p58).

- Broaden students' exploration: look at religious and political symbols and discuss their meanings and significance (*Man and his Symbols* edited by Carl Jung is a treasure trove of ideas on this subject). The symbolic meanings of dreams also makes for fascinating study. An excellent book on this topic is Tom Chetwynd's *Dictionary of Symbols*.

- Look at symbolism in heraldry. Students design their own shield or banner to sum up visually their attitudes to, for example, life, ambitions and desired goals.

- Look at how emotion symbols can be expressed in art, dance and drama. This might lead to further exploration of body language and how non-verbal communication is rich in signs and symbols.

Concept

Emotion theme cards

Being able to name emotions and notice differences between them is an important feature of EI. Emotions are investments of energy. When emotions are expressed, that energy rushes through us. We might be carried along passively in the rush – if the emotion is a positive one, perhaps no harm is done; but it can be destructive to be carried away by a seemingly negative feeling such as anger. Remember however the principle of positive intentions (see p10). That anger could be trying to say something useful. 'Reading the message' of the anger's energy and making choices about how to re-invest it indicate emotionally intelligent behaviour.

Application

Emotion theme cards (see below for an example) form a resource to help students 'read the feeling' more capably. Each card includes – the name of the emotion, an agreed symbol for it and or some other visual, such as people displaying that feeling, epithets and other quotes that provide an opportunity for reflection. The resource can be extended by pasting a theme card to a notebook, in which students can write (anonymously if necessary) about their experiences, share how they dealt with that feeling and offer advice to others.

Twinkle twinkle
Little star,
How I wonder
What you are

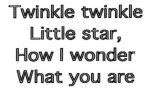

Wonder

Wonderful
Wonderland
Wonderment
Wondrous
Wonderkid

And still they gazed,
    and still the wonder grew,
That one small head
    could carry all he knew.
    Oliver Goldsmith

Concept

Mr Envy

Emotions help to make us what we are. Controlling our emotions helps to make us what we can be. Although emotions often evoke very physical responses (indeed, we might say that the emotions *are* the physical responses) they are also difficult to 'get a handle on' in terms of exploring and describing them. Ordinarily we engage with our feelings by expressing them. This is fine for positive emotions, but for negative or unpleasant feelings simply *being angry,* for instance, doesn't help us to talk about it or otherwise deal with it.

'Mr Envy' is a personification game that allows us to detach from the emotion we want to explore, understand and control.

TIP:
Older students too often love to draw. Boys especially (in my experience) enjoy illustrating their stories in 'Manga' style. This is ideal for the Mr Envy activity. If you are working with younger children, use Roger Hargreaves' *Mr Men* books as examples of personified emotions. Get the children to create new Mr Men characters based on other emotions.

Application

- Students work in pairs or small groups. Each group chooses an emotion to personify, for example envy, and discusses how an envious person might look. Students might want to mimic envy through facial expression and body posture, noticing small details. Now the group makes one or more drawings exaggerating the expression and posture that characterize envy. Once a number of these characters or caricatures have been created…

- Write letters and diary extracts from, for example, Mr Envy's point of view. Express his attitude to the world, his beliefs and values.

- Write or role-play dialogues between two or more personified emotions. What would Miss Optimistic say to Mr Envy?

- Ask older students to write fairy tales and parables where Mr Envy (and others), understands himself more deeply and learns how to change.

- In a drama workshop, ask students to take on the personifications – anchor positive emotions (see p52). Modify negative emotions by physically altering facial expression and body posture.

Mr Envy

Mr Pessimism

Concept

Control panel

Because thoughts, feelings and physical responses are connected, what and how we choose to think helps us to control our emotions. When I work creatively and therapeutically with people, I point out that using the imagination takes us into the world of make-believe. Then I explain that that means *making beliefs.* Consciously creating structures of thought – ideas, insights, intentions – serves to instruct the subconscious part of ourselves to react accordingly.

Control panel is a way of clearly setting up subconscious responses. It is an extension of the anchoring techniques we have already explored (see p52).

An example of a control panel

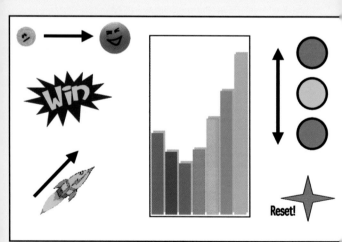

Application

■ Explain to students that they are going to draw a diagram of a control panel. This is not for controlling an aeroplane or space ship – it is to have more control over themselves. Once they have set the controls as they want them to be, students can then pretend (that is make believe) that the panel sends instructions through the brain to the body. They won't need to keep thinking about the control panel for it to keep working.

■ The panel illustrated is set up for a general intention – to remain focused, optimistic and confident, and to feel 'on the up'. Use the Reset button as a visual mental anchor. Whenever you want to 'refresh' that panel and remember* the feelings it controls, think of the Reset button and imagine pressing it.

■ Use the control panel technique to modify unhelpful feelings. Design the panel so that you can 'turn down' anger or lack of confidence, and so on. Have an 'On' button for calmness and self-assurance. Have a light that comes on or a buzzer that sounds if your body inadvertently returns to the posture that fits those feelings. Go through a visualization that sets up the panel just as you want it. Anchor those ideal settings with a Reset button.

* The word 'remember' means to re-create in the members – to bring back into the body – the positive feelings that (in this case) the control panel represents. Remembering is therefore not the same as recalling. To recall means to call information back from memory and bring it to conscious awareness. Remembering engages emotions and physical reactions.

Concept

Assertive rights

The *Concise Oxford English Dictionary* defines 'assert' as 'to declare, to insist upon one's rights' and states that assertiveness is linked to the idea of 'putting one's hand on a slave's head to free him'. The roots of the word lie with the Greek meaning 'to string together' as in 'a necklace'.

These ideas are powerful because when we assert ourselves we free ourselves from the slavery of intimidation and fear and our personalities become more integrated, as separate beads are threaded on a necklace. A classic book on the subject is Manuel J. Smith's *When I Say No I Feel Guilty*. Among the assertive rights that Smith identifies (and that you can use to positive effect in the classroom) are…

- The right to judge your own behaviour and to balance your rights with your responsibility to yourself and others.
- The right to change your mind (for reasons that you have considered).
- The right to make mistakes and be responsible for them.
- The right to say 'I don't know'.
- The right to say 'I don't understand'.

Note: Assertiveness is not aggressiveness. People are most empowered when insisting upon their assertive rights with calmness and confidence.

Application

- Build assertiveness training into ongoing PSHE and citizenship programmes. Post a 'Bill of Assertive Rights' in your classroom and make its use a high-profile part of classroom interaction.
- Use assertive rights as a tool in addressing any issue of bullying in the school.
- Use role play to encourage students to identify the difference between aggression and assertiveness, both in behaviour and language. For further ideas on this, see P. Baldwin's *With Drama in Mind: Real Learning in Imagined Worlds*.
- Make students aware that assertive people help themselves to become more confident and raise their self-esteem by –
  - Being clear and concise.
  - Being open and honest (take responsibility by using 'I' statements).
  - Being fair to yourself and other people.
  - Being direct and not avoiding issues.
  - Being prepared to listen, negotiate and compromise.
  - Being prepared to explore, experiment and try different strategies to resolve matters.

Concept

Parables

A parable is a 'wisdom tale', an apparently simple and even childlike story that has a magical quality rooted in symbol and metaphor. Parables are templates for human behaviour both on a personal and a social level. Such stories have been used since ancient times. A parable engages the listener on many levels: like all good stories they don't simply tell, but rather create experiences that allow the listener to enter a world of make-believe in order to learn new patterns and strategies. In the language of modern neuroscience, parables create neural pathways in the brain which help to shape our perception of the world and the way we interact with it.

Such simple stories can have a profound effect. I once worked with a girl who had a confidence problem. I asked her to imagine a pleasant place – she chose her back garden at home. I suggested that she could now notice something there that was relevant to her problem. Immediately she noticed a high brick wall and a football at her feet. She wanted to kick the ball, but it always bounced back off the wall. 'You're in the world of make-believe now,' I told her. 'Make the ball do something different.' At once, to the girl's delight, the ball grew wings. When she kicked it, it flew over the wall. 'I'm going to be the ball!' she said, and her arms extended as though she were flying. Then she looked at me, slightly embarrassed but pleased. 'I like that story,' she told me, 'It felt really good.'

It was a simple tale, but from that point onwards her confidence increased.

Increasingly, parables and similar stories are being used therapeutically. If you are interested in this field I recommend books such as *Stories for the Third Ear* by Lee Wallas and Arthur Rowshan's *Telling Tales*; also Pat Williams's tape lecture *How Stories Heal*. Pat also runs a course on this theme for the MindFields College (see References, p96).

Application

- Give students access to traditional parables and fairy tales. *Aesop's Fables* is an obvious example, but others from around the world are easily available in book form and on the internet.
- Ask students to make up their own parables, as a group or individually. I worked with a class of ten year olds and we made up a parable about bullying. It was called 'The Mini and the Juggernaut' – even though the juggernaut was so much bigger and scarier than the Mini and was quite intimidating, when the vehicles stopped at the motorway services and the drivers got out, the Mini driver was taller!
- Encourage students to read other activities in this book (such as Emotion theme cards (see p84) and Mr Envy (see p86) to give them ideas for parables. Keep these stories as a resource to tell to other groups.

TIP:
It's tempting to analyse parables for their meaning, but this isn't necessary for the stories to resonate in the listeners' minds and have beneficial effects.

Concept

Be here now

Imagine an hourglass with some of the sand left, but with some having fallen through into the bottom chamber. That hourglass is like a human life. The sand that has dropped through is the past. The sand that is yet to fall is the future (except that actually none of us knows how much sand remains). The neck of the hourglass represents our greatest treasure, this present moment – now, here. It is our only true point of interaction with reality.

So much emotional turmoil is created by projecting our imagination into the past or the future, which simply do not exist. The past has gone. All that remains of it is information lodged in our heads – our resource of memory and experience. The future likewise is nothing more than constructs of thought, which may or may not be borne out by what actually happens.

Although we can – and sometimes should – remember the past, to carry regrets serves no purpose. And although all of us wonder about the future, wishful thinking does not help to shape it in any meaningful way. Creating intentions generates motivation, but we can only make use of that energy now, in this present moment. Only by *realizing* (making real) that here-and-now is where our power lies, can we use both the past and the future most beneficially for our own well-being.

Application

- Set aside some time where you can work with your group undisturbed. Students can sit at their tables, or if you have a quiet open space available, you might prefer to use that. In this case students should sit cross-legged (using blankets and cushions as appropriate) in a relaxed but upright posture – not rigidly upright, not slouching.
- Spend a few minutes using breathing techniques to relax (see p21).
- Ask the students to begin noticing the thoughts that pass through their minds. Explain that you don't want them to think about anything in particular, but just to notice the thoughts that happen anyway – a bit like sitting on a riverbank watching the water flow by.
- After several minutes, put an object on display – an interesting stone, a flower, an ornament. Ask the students to rest their eyes on the object and also to imagine it. If their minds wander, they are to bring their thoughts back to the object. As an extension of this activity, you can suggest to students that they close their eyes and keep the object in their imagination.
- A few minutes later, with their eyes still resting on the object, ask your students to be aware of their own bodies. Just notice the position of the body as it sits relaxed and still.
- Now be aware of your body as part of the room (or open space) filled as it is with other people. Realize that you-here-now is the only thing that's truly real. You can only deal with one grain of sand at a time as it passes through the hourglass. This is the only place where you can have an influence. Let that idea soak into your mind.
- End the activity by letting students slowly stretch and yawn as they 'come back to themselves'.

References

Baldwin, P. (2004) *With Drama in Mind: Real Learning in Imagined Wor* ,
   Network Educational Press Ltd.

Bellanca, J. & Fogarty, R. (1995) *Teach Them Thinking*, IRI Skylight
   Training

Benson, H. (1976) *The Relaxation Response*, Harper Torch

Bowkett, S. (1999) *Self-Intelligence*, Network Educational Press

Bowkett, S. (2005) *100 Ideas for Teaching Creativity*, Continuum

Bowkett, S. (2006) *100 Ideas for Teaching Thinking Skills*, Continuum

Bowkett, S. (2006) *Pocket PAL: Boys and Writing*, Network Continuum
   Education

Buzan, T. (2000) *Head First,* Thorsons (plus many other books by
   this author)

Carnegie, D. (2007) *How to Win Friends and Influence People*, Vermillion

Chetwynd, T. (1993) *Dictionary of Symbols*, Aquarian Press

Claxton, G. (1997) *Hare Brain, Tortoise Mind*, Fourth Estate

Cohen, M. (2003) *101 Ethical Dilemmas*, Routledge

Day, J. (2006) *Creative Visualization With Children*, BookSurge Publishing

Dennison, P. E. & Dennison, G. E. (1987) *Edu-K for Kids* (a basic manual of
   Educational Kinesiology), Edu-Kinesthetics Inc.

Gardner, H. (1993) *Multiple Intelligences: the Theory in Practice*,
   Basic Books

Goleman, D. (2005) *Emotional Intelligence*, Bantam

Harris, C. (1999) *The Elements of NLP*, Element Books

Heller, S. & Steele, T. (2005) *Monsters and Magical Sticks*, New Falcon
   Publications

Hewitt, J. (1991) *The Complete Relaxation Book*, Rider & Co

James, T. & Woodsmall, W. (1988) *Time Line Therapy and the Basis of
   Personality*, Meta Publications

Jung, C. (1978) *Man and his Symbols*, Picador

Law, S. (2002) *The Philosophy Files* 1, Orion Children's Books

Law, S. (2006) *The Philosophy Files* 2, Orion Children's Books

Law, S. (2003) *The Philosophy Gym*, Headline Publishing

Lewis, B. & Pucelik, F. (1993) *Magic of NLP Demystified*, Metamorphosis
   Press

Markham, U. (1997) *The Elements of Visualization*, Element Books

O'Connor, J. & Seymour, J. (1993) *Introducing Neuro-Linguistic
   Programming*, Aquarian Press

Rossi, E. (1993) *The Psychobiology of Mind-Body Healing*, W. W. Norton
   & Co

Rowshan, A. (1997) *Telling Tales: how to Use Stories to Help Children Deal
   with the Challenges of Life*, Oneworld Publications

Smith, A. (2002) *Move It: Physical Movement and Learning,* Network
   Educational Press

Smith, M. J. (1975) *When I Say No I Feel Guilty*, Bantam Books

Stock, G. (1987) *The Book of Questions*, Workman Books

Wallas, L. (2004) *Stories for the Third Ear*, W. W. Norton & Co

Williams, P. (1998) *How Stories Heal*, European Therapy Studies Institute
   (ETSI): also The MindFields College, www.mindfields.org.uk

Woodhouse, S & Cheesbrough, M. (2006) *Helping Children with Yoga*,
   Continuum